D1085082

DISCARD

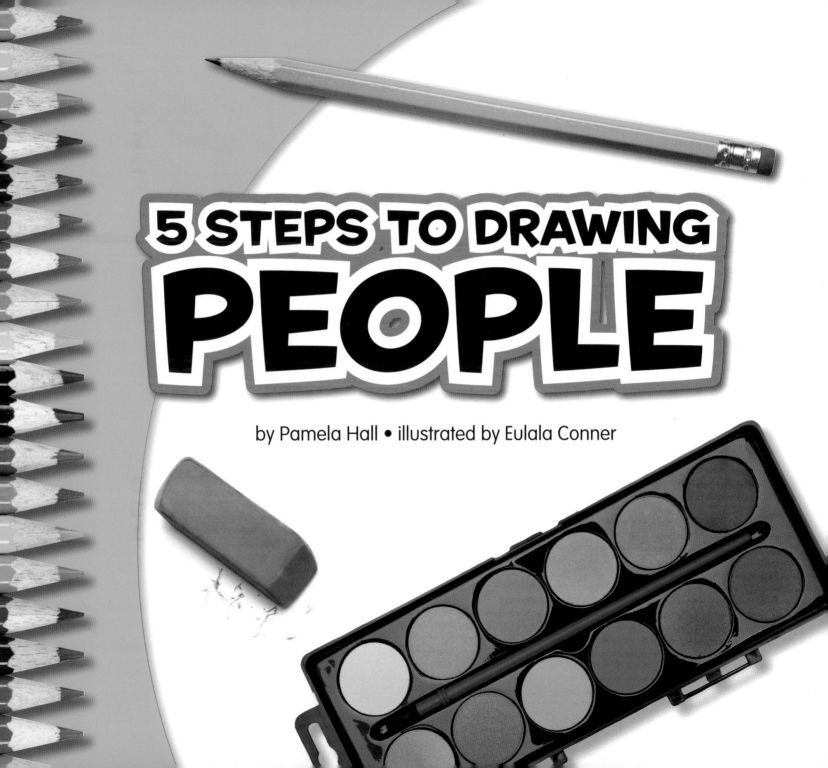

5 STEPS TO DRAWING
PEOPLE

by Pamela Hall • illustrated by Eulala Conner

The Child's
World

Published by The Child's World®
1980 Lookout Drive • Mankato, MN 56003-1705
800-599-READ • www.childsworld.com

ACKNOWLEDGMENTS
The Child's World®: Mary Berendes, Publishing Director
The Design Lab: Design and production
Red Line Editorial: Editorial direction

ISBN: 978-1-60973-203-5
LCCN: 2011927712

Printed in the United States of America
Mankato, MN
July 2011
PA02088

TABLE OF CONTENTS

ALL ABOUT GENES

There are billions of people in the world. New babies are born every second! Humans start out about the same size. Most weigh around 7 pounds (3.2 kg) when they are born.

But people change as they grow. Some people end up tall and thin. Others are short and squat. This is because of **genes**. Genes decide what a person's skin, hair, and eye color will be. These physical traits are

hereditary. That means your parents passed the genes down to you before you were born.

What about your **emotions** and skills? Are they passed down, too? Yes and no! Genes help shape your **personality** and skills. But your environment plays a big role, too. Environment is where you live and go to school. Environment helps figure out whether you will be shy or outgoing.

DIFFERENT FROM ANIMALS

How are humans different from animals? We walk on two legs. Our brains are more developed. We can question, reason, imagine, and plan.

Only humans are able to communicate with words. There are many different languages in the world. People speak Spanish, English, Arabic, Japanese, and many other languages. People who are deaf or have trouble hearing use American Sign Language.

Only humans laugh, too. We watch funny television shows and play tricks on each other. Some animals, like chimps and rats, do make sounds similar to laughter when tickled or played with. But they don't get jokes like humans do!

DIFFERENT AND ALIKE

People do things differently all over the world. **Cultures** are different. Some cultures celebrate different holidays and wear special clothing. Things we eat are very different. Our homes are different, too. Some people live in simple huts. Others live in huge mansions.

Families are different. Some families have two parents. Others have one. Some families may have aunts, uncles, and grandparents living together. Some people live alone.

But people are alike in many ways. We all need food, water, and shelter. We have similar fears, hopes, and dreams. We work and play, too. Most of us like to be around other people at least sometimes.

DRAWING TIPS

You've learned about people. You're almost ready to draw them. But first, here are a few drawing tips:

Every artist needs tools. To learn how to draw people, you will need:

- Some paper
- A pencil
- An eraser
- Markers, crayons, colored pencils, or watercolors (optional)

Anyone can learn to draw. You might think only some people can draw. That's not true. Everyone can learn to draw. It takes practice, though. The more you draw, the better you will be. With practice, you will become a true artist!

Everyone makes mistakes. This is okay! Mistakes help you learn. They help you know what not to do next time. Mistakes can even make your drawing more special. It's all right if you draw a person's legs too long. Now you've got a one-of-a-kind drawing. You can erase a mistake you don't like, too. Then start again!

Stay loose. Relax your body before you begin. Hold your pencil lightly. Don't rest your wrist on the table. Instead, move your whole arm as you draw. This will help you make smooth lines. Press lightly on the paper when you draw or erase.

Drawing is fun! The most important thing about drawing is to have fun. Be creative. Your drawings don't have to look exactly like the pictures in this book. Try changing the position of a person's arms. You can also use markers, crayons, colored pencils, or watercolors to bring your people to life.

1

2
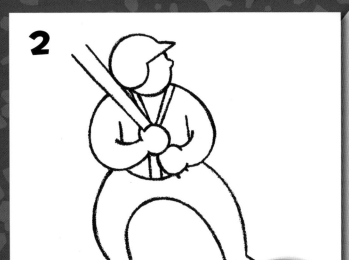

BASEBALL PLAYER

3

4

Baseball is one of the most popular sports in the United States. Not all baseball players earn money to play. Many people play for fun, too.

1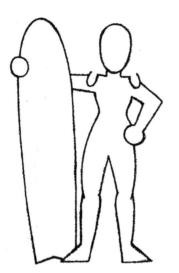

2

SURFER GIRL

3

4

A surfer girl finds big waves. Then she rides on her board to the shore. Riding on the crest of a wave is exciting. But a surfer must be careful. She watches out for waves that are too big.

1

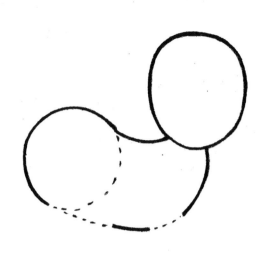

2

BABY

3

4

A baby sleeps up to 16 hours a day. A baby starts to smile at about one month old. He or she laughs at around four months. Rolling over, crawling, walking, and talking come next.

5

1

2

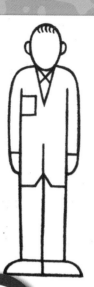

DOCTOR

3

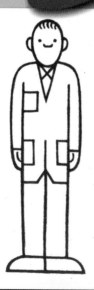

4

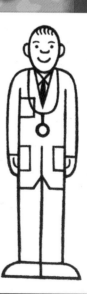

Doctors must go to school for a long time to learn how to take care of our bodies. Some doctors help kids. Others help people who got hurt playing sports. Some help us when we feel sad.

1

2

ROCK STAR

3

4

Rock stars play music during rock concerts. They work hard to be good at singing, writing songs, and playing their instruments.

1

2

PILOT

3

4

Pilots fly aircraft. Many pilots fly passenger planes. These pilots get people safely from one place to another. Pilots watch the weather very carefully.

5

1

2

MOVIE STAR

3

4

Movie stars play characters in a story. Some movie stars make a lot of money. Some people like to read about the lives of movie stars in magazines.

1

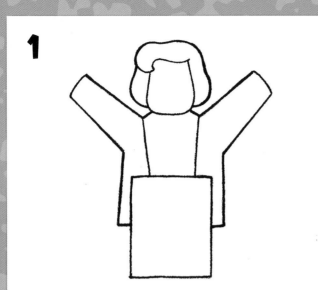

2

PRESIDENT

3

4

A president is the leader of a country. Countries around the world have had female presidents. These countries include Brazil, Liberia, and Lithuania. The United States may have a female president someday, too.

MORE DRAWING

Now you know how to draw people. Here are some ways to keep drawing them.

People come in different shapes and sizes. You can draw them all! Try using pens or colored pencils to draw and color in details. Experiment with crayons and markers to give your drawings different colors. You can also paint your drawings. Watercolors are easy to use. If you make a mistake, you can wipe it away with a damp cloth. Try tracing the outline of your drawing with a crayon or a marker. Then paint over it with watercolor. What happens?

Drawing Real People

When you want something new to draw, just look around. People are everywhere. Sit on a park bench or at a baseball game. Find someone interesting to draw. First, look at the person carefully. Is he or she tall or short? What kind of hair does he or she have? Now try drawing! If you need help, use the examples in this book to guide you.

GLOSSARY

cultures (KUL-churs): Cultures are ways of life, ideas, and traditions of a group of people. There are many cultures throughout the world.

emotions (ih-MOH-shuns): Emotions are strong feelings, such as happiness, love, and anger. The emotions people feel can be affected by events that happen around them.

genes (JEENS): Genes are parts of cells that carry information about how you look and grow. Genes determine if a baby will be a boy or a girl.

hereditary (huh-RED-uh-ter-ee): If something is hereditary, it is passed from parent to child. Eye color is hereditary.

personality (pur-suh-NAL-uh-tee): A personality is all the qualities and traits that make a person different from another. Someone can have a shy or talkative personality.

FIND OUT MORE

BOOKS

Emberley, Ed. *Ed Emberley's Drawing Book: Make a World*. New York: Little Brown, 2006.

Gravel, Elise. *Let's Draw and Doodle Together*. Maplewood, NJ: Blue Apple Books, 2010.

Smith, David J. *If America Were a Village: A Book about the People of the United States*. Toronto: Kids Can Press, 2009.

WEB SITES

Visit our Web site for links about drawing people:

childsworld.com/links

Note to Parents, Teachers, and Librarians: We routinely verify our Web links to make sure they are safe and active sites. So encourage your readers to check them out!

INDEX

ABOUT THE AUTHOR:
Pamela Hall lives near the St. Croix River in Lakeland, Minnesota, with her children and dog. Along with writing for children, Pamela enjoys being outdoors and feeding wildlife.

ABOUT THE ILLUSTRATOR:
Eulala Conner lives in Westport, Connecticut. She uses a combination of colorful dyes and watercolors over a line drawing to make her vibrant work come alive.